The New Passion of Playing Bass

By Peter Washburne

Online Audio

www.melbay.com/30566MEB

www.melbay.com

Contents

Preface

How is this bass book different? The energetic style, the particular grooves, the virtuoso musicianship coupled with the technical dexterity will empower, impassion and encourage bass players to play more creatively and realize remarkable improvement and foster more enthusiasm for this amazing instrument.

Grack, (Pete Washburne), was born in a suburb of Detroit, Michigan, and has played bass for over forty-four years, and lived in Europe for more than half his life, and his aim is to share his passion for playing bass with the world.

The aim of the original compositions is to create musical images of people and places. Thus, while the tune is played and replayed the original sense impressions of the source of inspiration are recreated in the mind of the composer.

Where does the motivation come from and how does he create his original musical compositions? He says:

"How can I create new sounds—different than other bassists? Well, I found a way: approach playing the bass with a different technique and a different fingering approach. My bass guitar teacher, Mr. Joe Fava Jr., of Detroit, Michigan taught me how to develop and utilize the little finger more dominantly for left hand fingerings.

"On many occasions I've held my bass out at arm's length, looked at it and asked "if it could sing, what would it sing?" or "how can I bring out the most interesting sounding new bass line from this bass?"

"How can I express the impressions (or vibrations of sound) impressed upon my mind from a person, a place, a thing or an experience? I elicit the sounds from my fingers and my bass because I first get an impulse of thought and I transmute, or convert this impulse of thought into a musical note, and then my fingers lead themselves to the notes that give the sound—or close to the sound I envision in my head."

Pete Washburne

Pasqua

Peter Washburne

D.C. al Fine
D.C. al Fine
Fine
Fine

Autumn Groove

Peter Washburne

Tempo 150

Tempo 144
1.
2.
Tempo 150

Fine
Fine

Teen Talk

Peter Washburne

Tempo 138

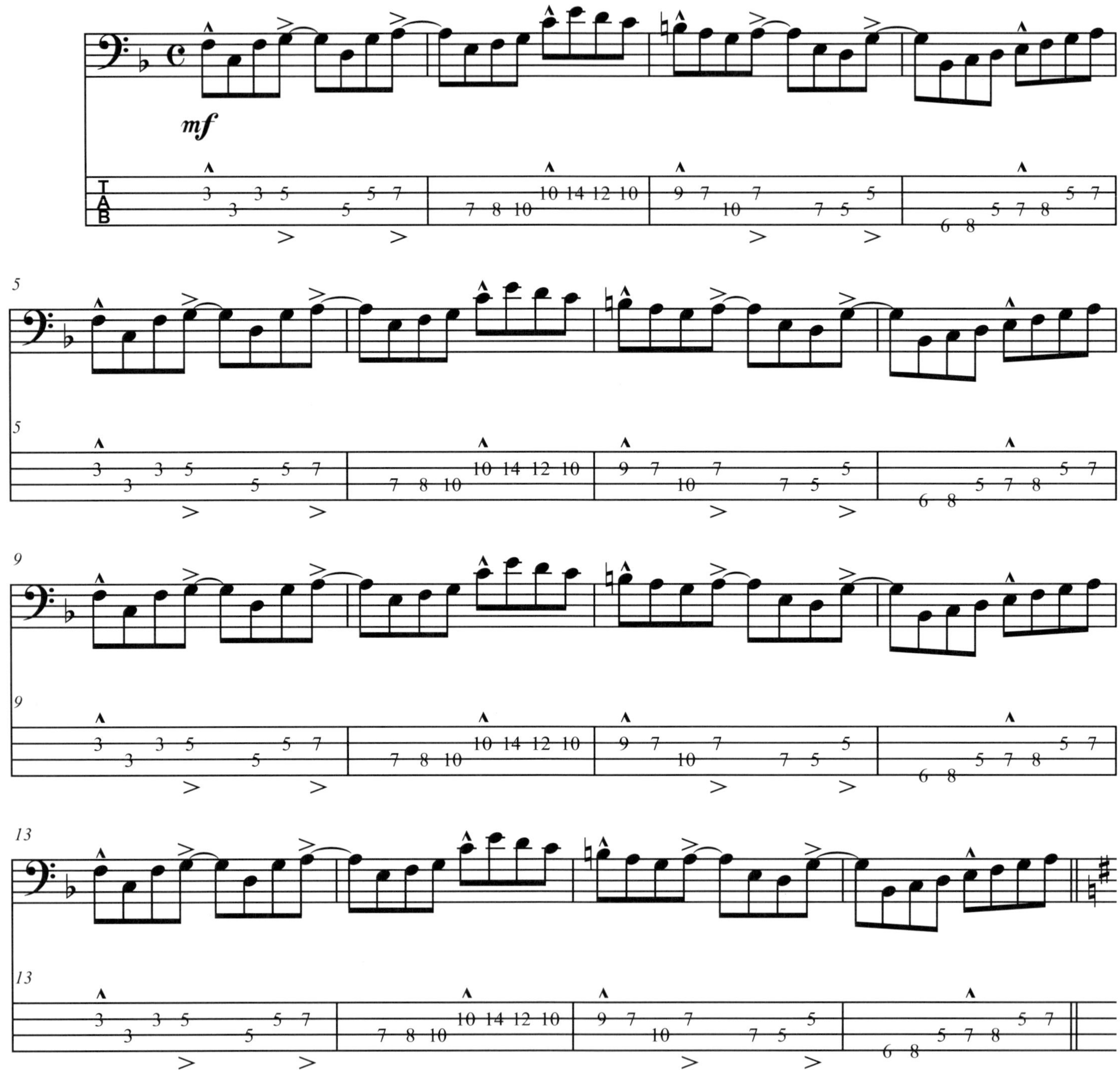

mp

38
42
46
1.
2.
51
mf

55
59
63
Fine
Fine

DTM

Peter Washburne

Tempo 152

17
21
25
28
32
D.C. al Fine

D.C. al Fine
D.C. al Fine

Portrait of Ada

Peter Washburne

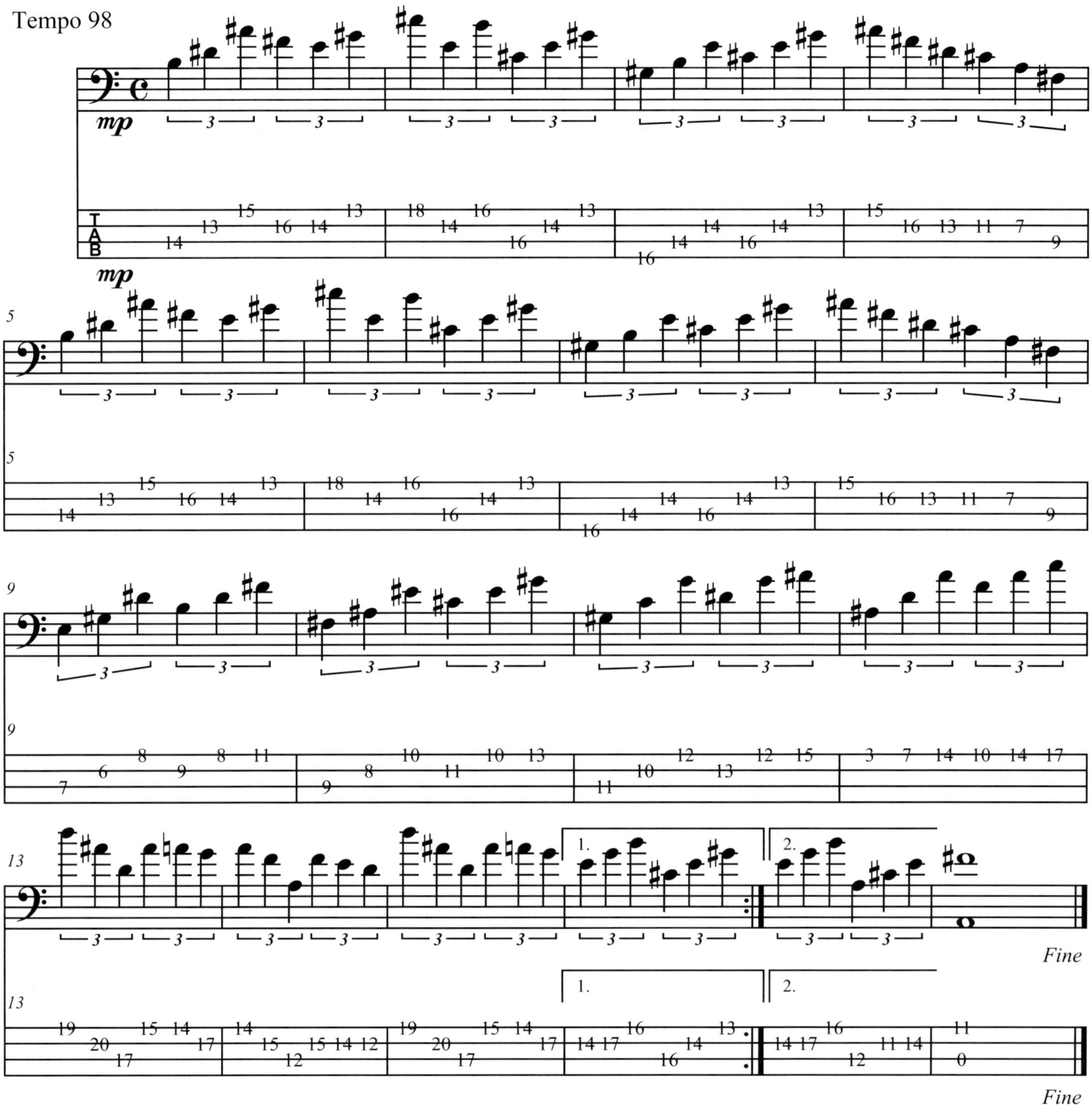

Pullin for Joe

Peter Washburne

D.S. al Coda
D.S. al Coda

57
61
Fine
Fine

Peter Gee

Peter Washburne

Tempo 174

Gliss.
Fine

Major Thirds

Peter Washburne

Tempo 96

13
13
16
16
19
19
22
22
25
25

28
28
1.
2.
30
Fine
1.
2.
30
Fine

Bass Solo No. 3

Peter Washburne

Tempo 144

37
37
41
41
45
45
49
49

Tempo 100

Tempo 132
mf
mf
D.C. al Fine
D.C. al Fine

About the Author

Peter Gratiot Washburne, (nicknamed "Grack") was born in January 1957 in Detroit, Michigan and grew up listening to Motown and Detroit rock bands and became especially keen on progressive rock. He took up the bass guitar at age 15 and started playing in various rock bands in Detroit suburbs (and performed the upright bass in the High School orchestra for two years) until 1977 when he enlisted as a competent, professional musician in the U.S. Navy.

Peter performed world-wide in combos and big bands, jazz trios and quartets for over eight years, demonstrating and continually developing his skill at performing a wide variety of musical styles from Latin to Greek, Ballads to Funk, Blues to Dixie, Disco to the innovative music of the jazz group Weather Report. In addition, Peter wrote original compositions and learned how to compose music scores for big bands

While performing the electric bass as a member of the Navy Band, Peter did a 17 month gig on Guam and then toured Europe, Asia, Great Britain, the Middle East and North Africa, and much of Italy. After retirement from the Navy, Peter continued to explore and develop his passion for his bass guitar hobby by playing at home on his personal collection of over five different hand-selected electric basses.

Additionally, Peter has travelled to over 32 countries throughout the world, speaks five languages, knows 'language pleasantries' in over 12 different languages—so he has become inundated with cultural richness as a spin-off of his experiences abroad—and this cultural heritage is reflected in his rhythms and melodies.

Peter has amassed a remarkable collection of over 310 original etudes, bass solos, band backing tracks and cool riffs housed in his seven (7) un-published music books.

This is Peter's first published collection.

Peter Washburne

WWW.MELBAY.COM